CHOOSING
BRAVE

HOW MAMIE TILL-MOBLEY AND EMMETT TILL SPARKED THE CIVIL RIGHTS MOVEMENT

ANGELA JOY

ILLUSTRATED BY JANELLE WASHINGTON

ROARING BROOK PRESS
NEW YORK

August 31, 1955

The boy they found was far from home,
far from Mother and Grandmother.
"Here on a visit," Papa Mose would say.
The sheriff set out to dig a grave that day,
to hide the crime in the mud of Mississippi,
where no one would see the boy's suffering.
But Mamie did the harder thing.
She said, "No. You send my son home."

It was the braver thing
that changed everything.

Mamie Elizabeth Carthan was a child of the Great Migration,
up from Mississippi with her family
in search of a better life:
a life with a little less fear,
a life with a little more freedom.

Daddy found work in Argo, outside of Chicago, making all sorts of things from corn:

corn oil, corn binding, corn syrup, cornstarch.

But on the weekends, he made music

at the juke joint on Forty-Third . . .

The patrons paid in whiskey, though,

making it hard to go to work

come Monday.

Mama didn't care for juke joints. Her joy was Jesus, food, and family:

"Fish fry! Lemon pie! Y'all come on and eat."

All were welcome at Mama's table: neighbors and pastors, strangers and friends,

those who were saved and those who needed saving—

from sin,

from the South.

They gathered there . . .

The sugar fluff of Mama's meringue cut the bitterness of thick-spun stories . . .

all about Jim Crow.

Easy to get arrested.

Hard to find a job.

Hard to feel safe, sometimes.

Mamie was glad to be in Argo, outside of Chicago,

where a girl could roam free.

But that didn't mean life was easy.

Eleven years old was hard.

Daddy pressed a Buffalo nickel in the palm of Mamie's hand

and walked away.

He never did come back.

Fourteen was hard.

Boys in school were cruel, and not every teacher was kind.

Still, Mamie found comfort in her studies:

science, Latin, geometry, poetry—reliable subjects.

Loyal. True.

Diploma in hand, Mamie was unusual indeed:

the first African American to graduate at the top of her class.

Yet the best of grades couldn't hush what she heard on street corner and pew:

"Can't catch a man with a book," they said. "Better marry somebody soon."

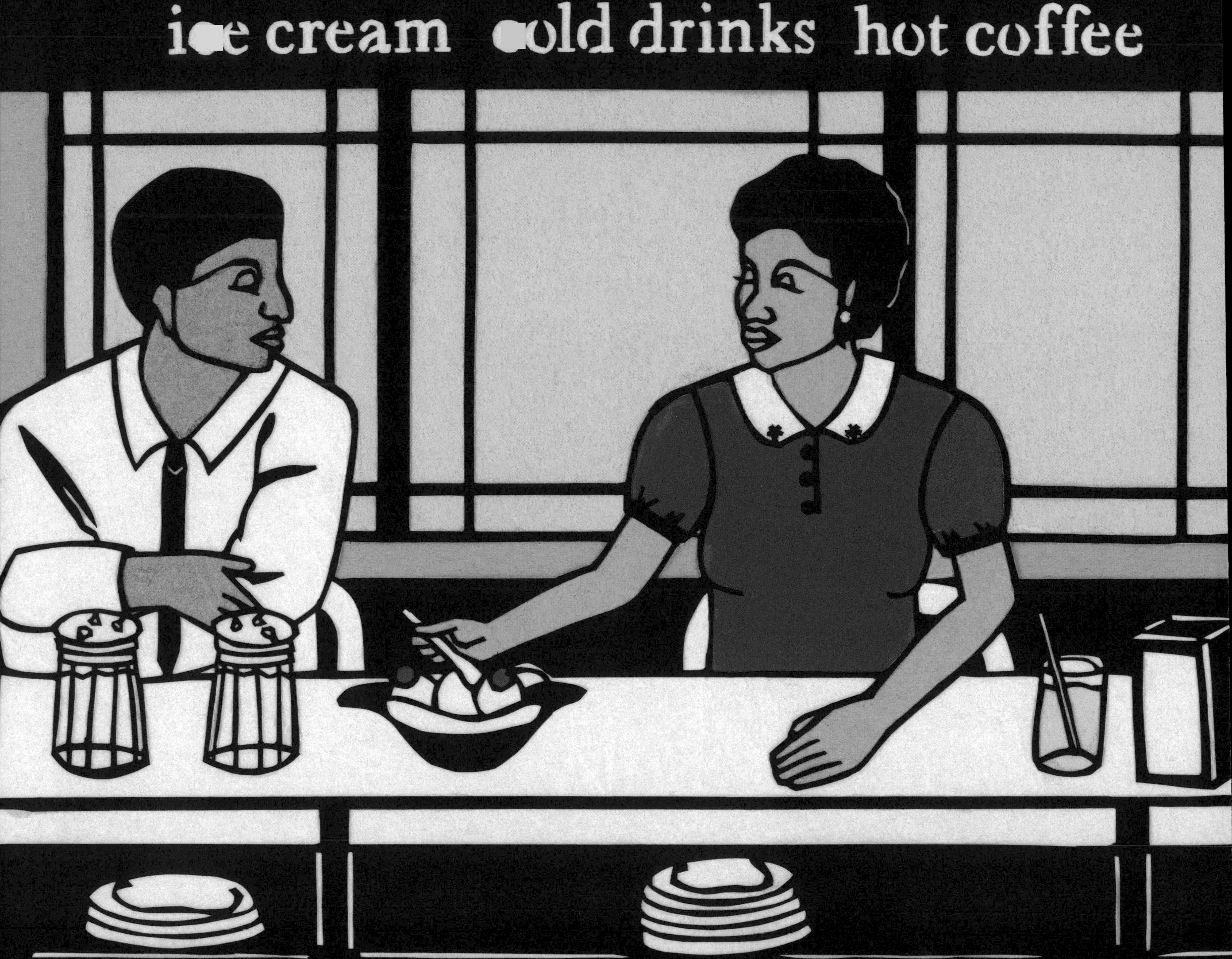
ice cream cold drinks hot coffee

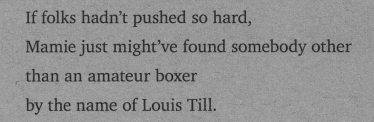

If folks hadn't pushed so hard,
Mamie just might've found somebody other
than an amateur boxer
by the name of Louis Till.

Louis came 'round and around Mamie's porch
'til Mama finally let her go—
just up the street,
just for a banana split.

Mamie wasn't aware that Louis planned on eating there—
right in the middle of all those white folks!
That's not how it worked, not even in Argo, outside of Chicago,
where a girl could roam free.

The owner was furious—Mama would be, too.
Yet, while still afraid, Mamie stayed.
It was the braver thing.

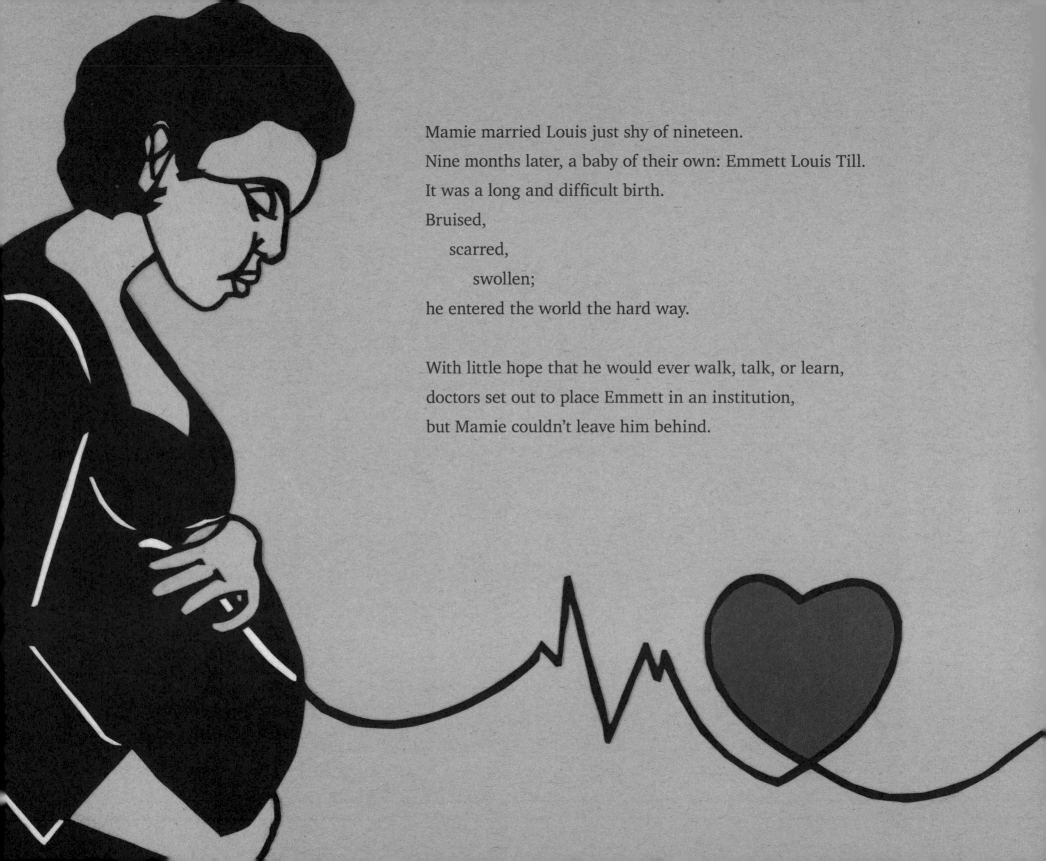

Mamie married Louis just shy of nineteen.

Nine months later, a baby of their own: Emmett Louis Till.

It was a long and difficult birth.

Bruised,

    scarred,

       swollen;

he entered the world the hard way.

With little hope that he would ever walk, talk, or learn,

doctors set out to place Emmett in an institution,

but Mamie couldn't leave him behind.

She had to bring her baby home.
It was the harder thing.

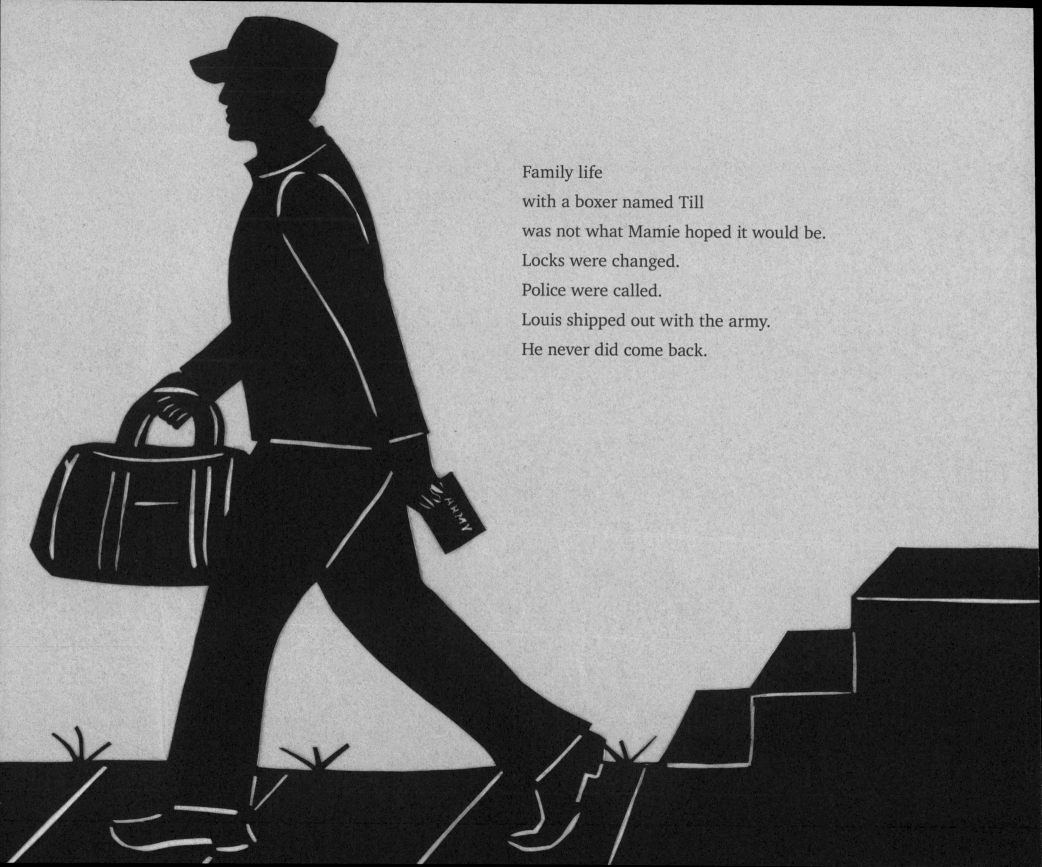

Family life

with a boxer named Till

was not what Mamie hoped it would be.

Locks were changed.

Police were called.

Louis shipped out with the army.

He never did come back.

A telegram and silver ring were safely tucked away—
they'd be Emmett's one day:
fragments of a father
he'd never have the chance to know.

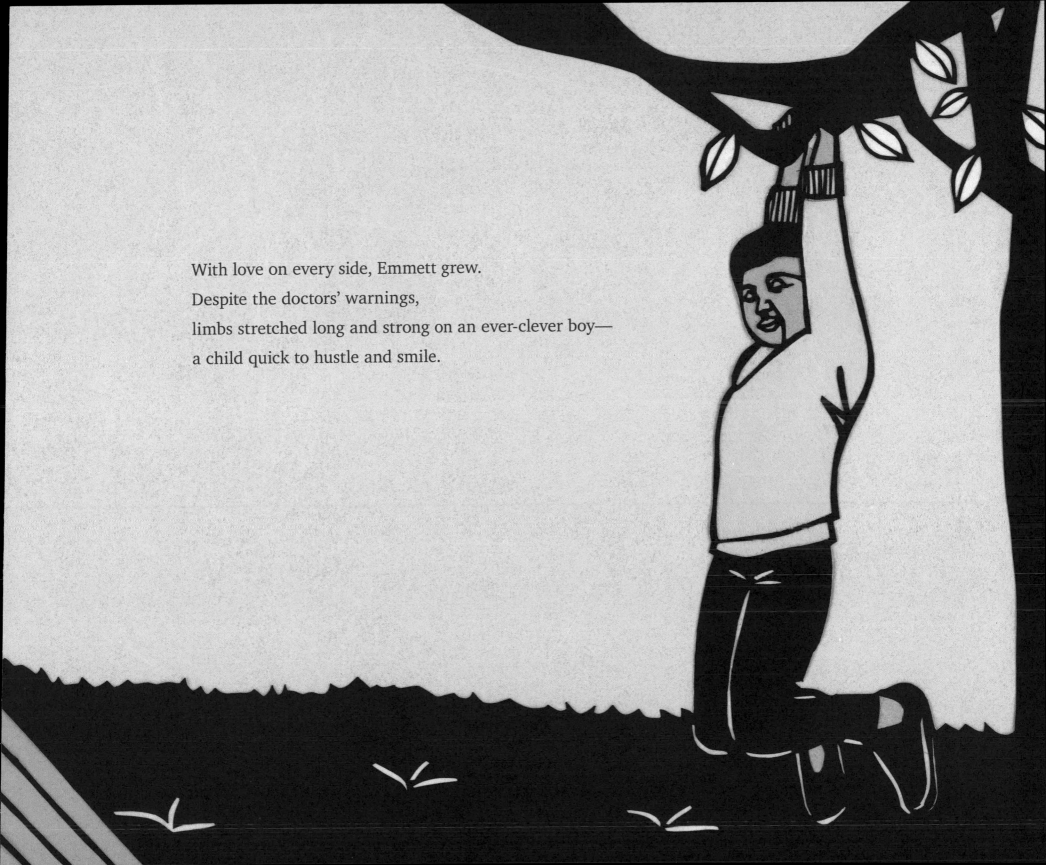

With love on every side, Emmett grew.

Despite the doctors' warnings,

limbs stretched long and strong on an ever-clever boy—

a child quick to hustle and smile.

When the milkman came, Emmett collected bottles.

The work was hard, but the reward was sweet.

When the iceman came, Emmett ran ahead.

The quarter he earned felt cool on summer skin.

Wrapped in the arms of Argo,
outside of Chicago,
Emmett roamed free.

It was strange, then, when he came in before sunset,
asking to rest awhile.
Mamie tried everything she knew,
but when Emmett didn't get any better, she sent for help.
The doctor called it "polio."
There was no cure.
All Mamie could do
was pray.

With steadfast faith and tender care, Emmett did recover,
but the polio left a scar—
an invisible reminder—
a stutter of speech.
From time to time,
Emmett's tongue and mind got stuck on words like
"bubble gum,"
"soda pop,"
or "MoonPie."

But Mamie found a trick—a work-around:
She told him to stop,
take a breath,
and whistle.
Whistling calmed Emmett,
steadied him,
allowing him to finish what he started to say.

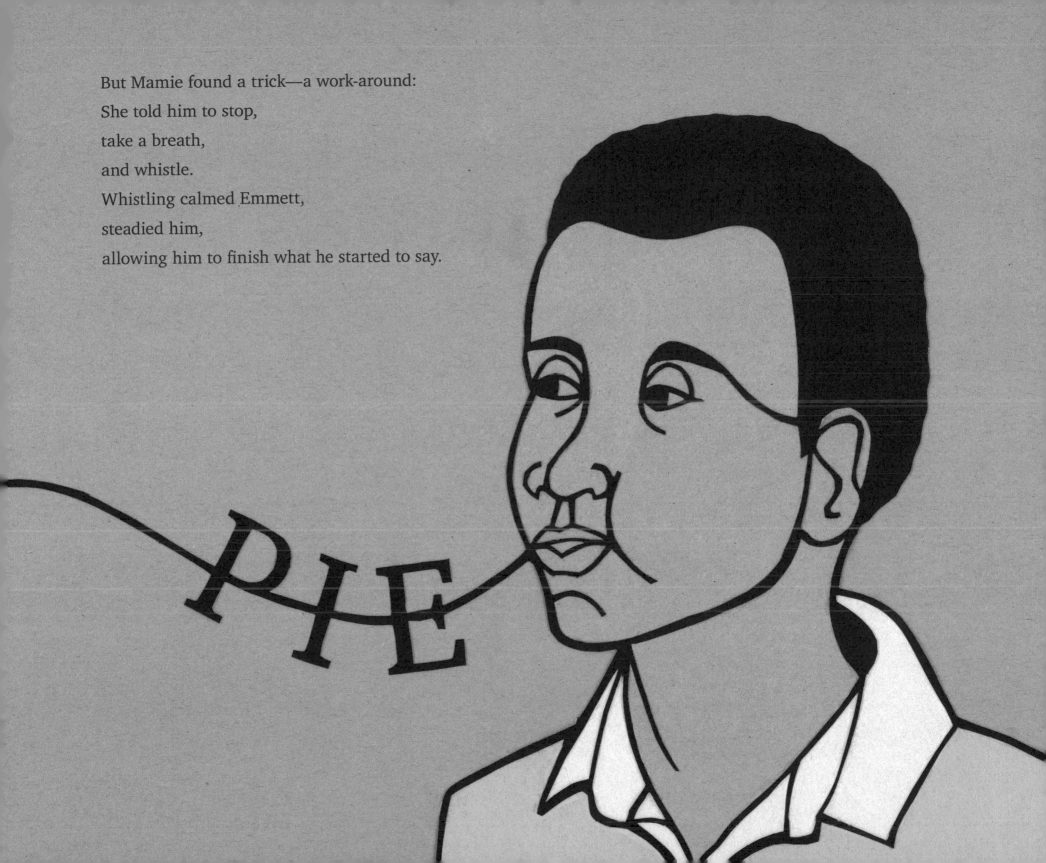

With time, talent, and plenty of hard work,
a new life came calling for Mamie—
life in the BIG city: Chicago.
Emmett was so proud of his mama.
Together they made a great team.

But deep inside
he missed Argo, *outside* of Chicago.
He missed wide-open spaces,
the freedom to run.
He missed neighbors and pastors,
family and friends.

So when the invitation came to go south—

SOUTH to fishing in the Delta,

SOUTH to mud-hole days,

SOUTH to more cousins than he could ever fit in his upstairs apartment—

Emmett was eager to go.

But Mamie said, "No."

The laws of Jim Crow made it un*safe*

for Black boys

to roam free.

Still, Emmett made his case:

He was a smart boy.

He had good manners.

Surely she could trust Papa Mose and Aunt Lizzie!

Finally,

with a worried heart,

Mamie agreed.

Sometimes a mother gets a feeling, an ache deep down in her soul—a warning.

With Emmett's kiss still fresh on Mamie's cheek, the train wailed.

Something awful was coming.

Something Mamie could not stop.

One week
and one day
after Emmett boarded the Mississippi train,
an early-morning phone call . . .
words on the line that didn't make sense at all . . .
Emmett was missing—stolen in the night.
No one could say where he was.

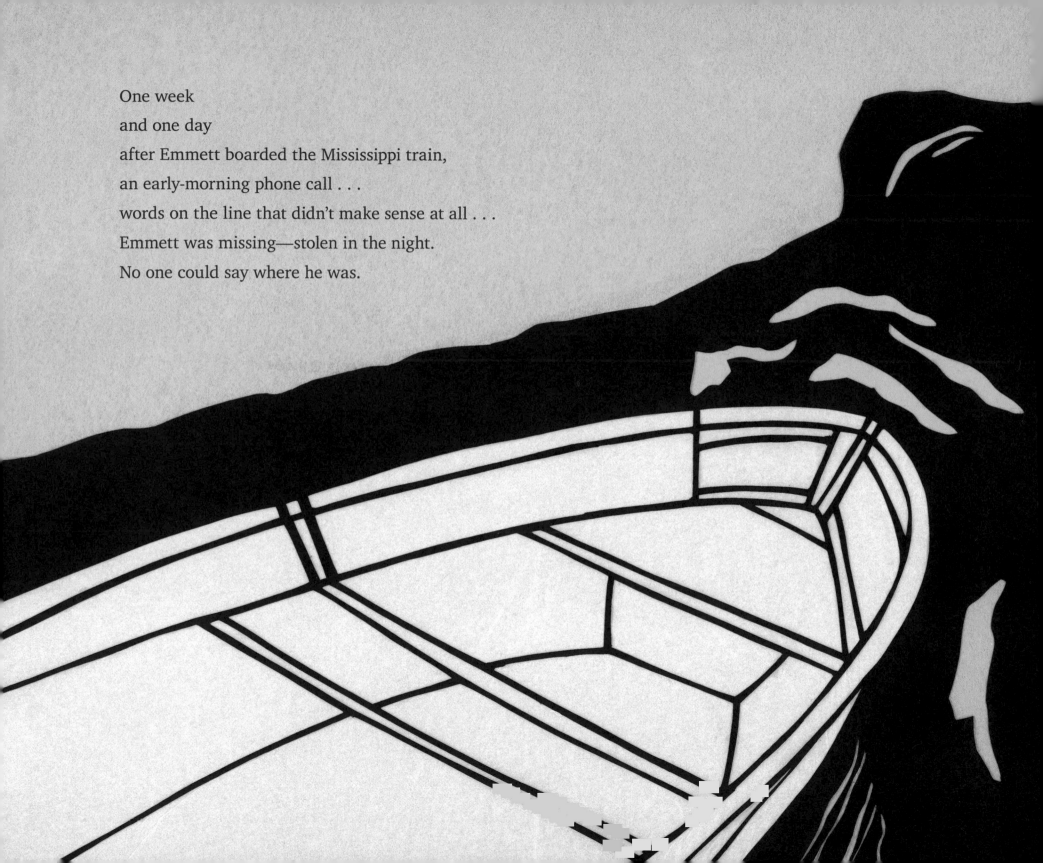

It was three days before fishermen found Emmett
in the Tallahatchie:

bruised,
    scarred,
        swollen.

He left the world the hard way . . .

        The laws of Jim Crow made it un*safe*
            for Black boys
                to roam free . . .

It started with a whistle.

The kind of whistle white women called rude

and white men called profane.

It started with a whistle.

The story that

   shifted

         over

            time

from a forgotten "Ma'am" to something far worse—

it started with a whistle.

The lie that brought killers to Emmett's bedroom door:

Praise for a smooth checkers move?

A poorly timed joke?

A work-around for a stuttering boy bragging on bubble gum?

It started with a whistle—

one breath; one sound; one moment

to seal the fate of Emmett Till.

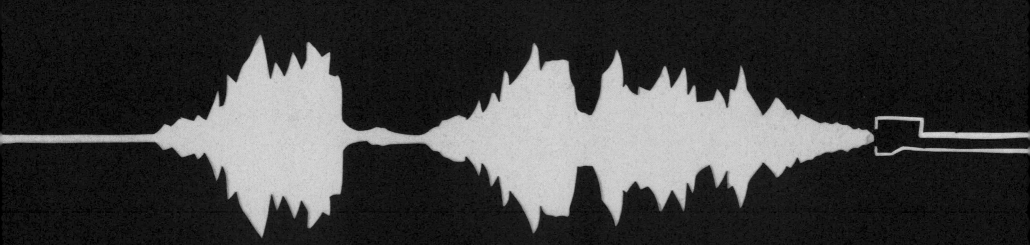

The sheriff set out to dig a grave *that day*,
to hide the crime in the mud of Mississippi,
where no one would see the boy's suffering.
But Mamie said, "No."
The land that killed him
would not keep him.
She had to bring her baby home.

At a cost of more than Mamie could earn in a year,
the wailing train that carried Emmett south
brought him home, again.

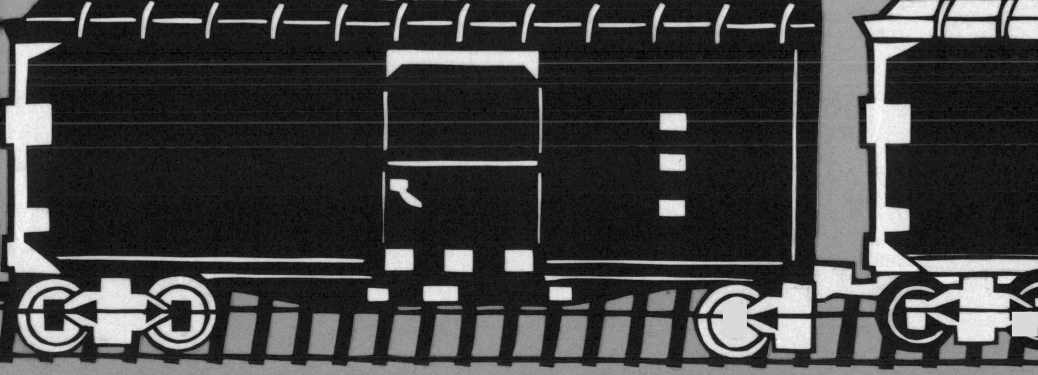

The casket arrived locked in a box—
a box that had no key;
a box with legal papers forbidding anyone to open
what the state of Mississippi held shut.

But Mississippi had no power—not here.
That box was coming open.
Mamie *had* to see her son.

It was the harder thing.

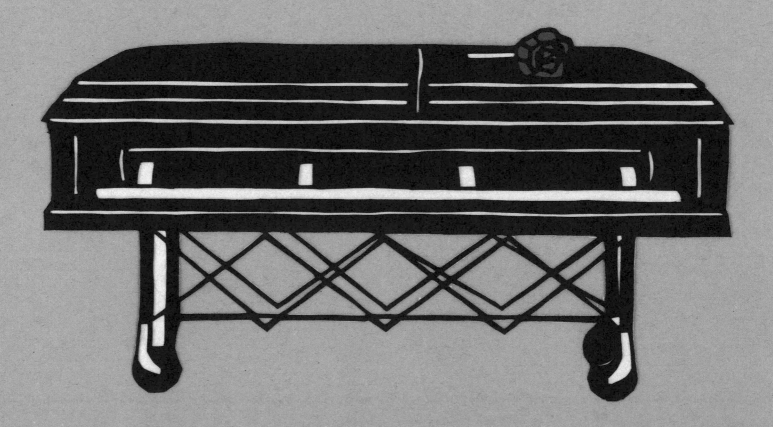

The haircut—still fresh from the barber.
The curve of ankle, strength of thigh.
The silver ring . . . his father's silver ring.
Yes, that was Emmett, but only Mamie would know.

His skin,
his smile,
his ears,
his eyes:
ruined.

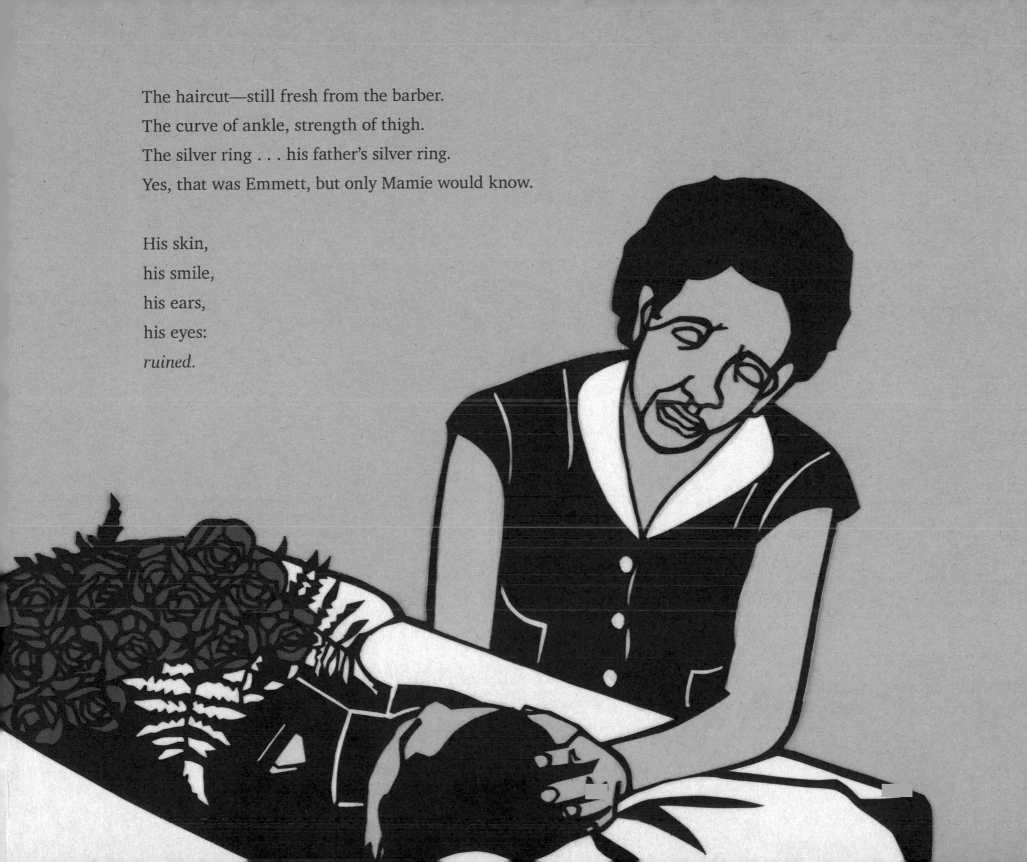

It would have been easy, then, to go to sleep beside him;

to save her pain for privacy;

to bury Emmett quietly.

But Mamie did the braver thing.

She sounded the alarm.

For four long days, she let the people come:

to bear witness,

to mourn the son erased for the "sin" of a sound:

a stutter,

a whistle,

a laugh.

Reporters came, too, to tell Emmett's story—to document Emmett's pain.

The image, reprinted on smooth and glossy papers,

said more with a flash than ten thousand words;

lighting a match

to a Civil Rights Movement

long-primed

to blow.

City to city,

town to town,

people stood up,

and Rosa, sweet Rosa, sat down.

The murder trial was set for Sumner, Mississippi.
Mamie made her way.
Fathers with sons
aimed fingers and guns
at Mamie as she passed by.
Yet, while still afraid, Mamie stayed.

Seated in hot and segregated spaces,
Mamie suffered the *in*justice.

Sixty minutes and a soda break
brought the all-white jury to its decision:
not guilty.
Twelve men and a judge set murderers free.
A second murder mourned—
the death of decency.

Joined by the NAACP, Mamie traveled to rallies near and far,

calling for justice—

not just for Emmett, but for sons and daughters still living:

using brokenness to build,

pain

to heal.

But all too soon,

that, too,

came to an end.

With new headlines to write,

new battles to fight,

the world moved on without Mamie.

The world moved on without Emmett.

The home they shared grew painfully quiet . . .

Yet Mamie couldn't wither.
It wasn't her way.
Grasping at what she *knew* to be true—
science, Latin, geometry, poetry—
Mamie returned to school.

While studying to be a teacher,
Mamie married Emmett's longtime barber and friend, Gene Mobley,
a gentle man who stood with Mamie
through the ugliest days.
He never walked away.
Together, they made a patchwork family
to warm the place where Emmett used to be.

In the years that followed, Mamie poured *life* and *love* into community:

helping students no one else could reach,

visiting the victims of violence,

working for social change.

She taught the speeches of Dr. King to young performers after school.

She called them the Emmett Till Players.

In turn, they called her

Mother Mobley.

Together they traveled the country,

winning honor and applause along the way.

In 2003, at the age of eighty-one, Mamie Till-Mobley passed away.

Thousands came to celebrate her achievements—

to lay a hero to rest.

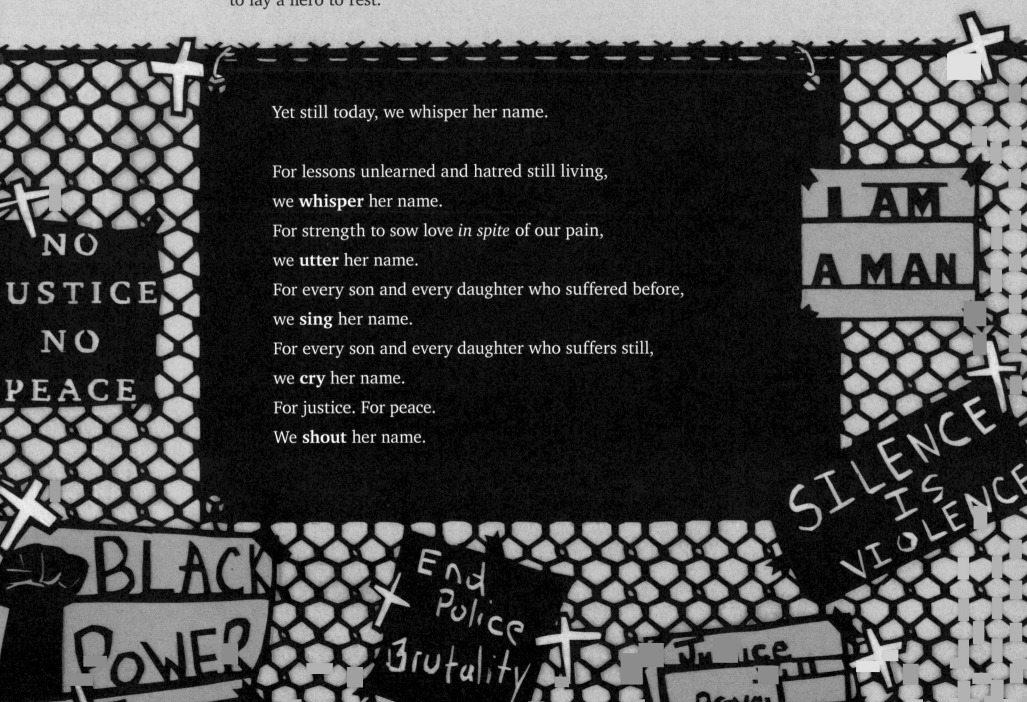

Yet still today, we whisper her name.

For lessons unlearned and hatred still living,
we **whisper** her name.
For strength to sow love *in spite* of our pain,
we **utter** her name.
For every son and every daughter who suffered before,
we **sing** her name.
For every son and every daughter who suffers still,
we **cry** her name.
For justice. For peace.
We **shout** her name.

For Emmett . . .

Let the people see what I have seen.
We have averted our eyes far too long.
Everybody needs to know what happened to
Emmett Till.
—Mamie Till-Mobley

Trayvon Martin

James Byrd Jr.

Jordan Davis

Tamir Rice

Oscar Grant

Richard Collins III

Elijah McClain

Eric Garner

Philando Castile

The Charleston AME 9

Amadou Diallo

Atatiana Jefferson

Darius Simmons

Renisha McBride

Timothy Caughman

Botham Jean

Patrick Warren

Ahmaud Arbery

Breonna Taylor

George Floyd Jr.

Author's Note

The original Mother of the Movement, Mamie Elizabeth Carthan, was born near Webb, Mississippi, on November 23, 1921. Two years later, as part of the Great Migration, the Carthan family left Mississippi, fleeing the highest rate of documented lynching in the country. They settled in a small Illinois town by the name of Argo. Yet the family's move north unwittingly set into motion the very violence they were hoping to escape.

Growing up, Mamie was smart, hardworking, and determined, remaining in school long after many of her contemporaries left to work or get married. As proud as neighbors and family members were of Mamie's accomplishments—she was the first African American to make the honor roll and the first to graduate top of the class—they didn't know how to make room for an intelligent, independent, *single* woman. Mamie was eighteen now—practically an "Old Maid." She was expected to marry, so she did. As it turned out, Louis Till, the amateur boxer who had courted Mamie, also had little interest in becoming a spouse. Still, gambling, drinking, and staying out late would have to be tolerated. They had a baby on the way, but when Louis became physically violent, Mamie knew he had to go. Refusing his attempts to apologize, she called the police and changed the locks. Louis was arrested and charged with assault.

The judge gave Louis a choice: go to jail or enlist in the army. Louis chose the latter, rendering Mamie a widow. At the age of twenty-three, Mamie was left with no military benefits and a son to raise alone. All she received in the mail was a telegram and a few of Louis's possessions, including a silver ring—the same ring that would be used years later to identify their disfigured son as he was pulled from the Tallahatchie River.

With Louis gone, Mamie had no choice but to enter the workforce. Luckily, her education served her well. With a position as a clerk-typist at the Coffey School of Aeronautics, Mamie made good money while her mother watched the baby. Together they raised a healthy, intelligent, charismatic boy: Emmett Louis Till.

When Emmett disappeared on August 28, 1955, Mamie, with admirable composure, stood in front of the press to tell the story. This single act put reputation, livelihood, and life at risk. Yet Mamie could not allow her son to disappear in the middle of a Mississippi night without a fight. Against conventions of the time, Mamie spoke out: first for help, then for justice. Rosa Parks was one of the many who heard. On November 27, 1955, Mrs. Parks attended a meeting in Montgomery, Alabama, to discuss the horrific murder of Emmett Till. Just four days later, disgusted by the status quo, Rosa refused to give up her seat and move to the back of the bus. Later, when the two women met, Rosa told Mamie that she thought of Emmett as she sat waiting to be arrested. Rosa spoke of how important Emmett was to her, speaking woman to woman, mother to mother. In retrospect, we now understand that it was the synergy of these women's actions that ignited the modern Civil Rights Movement.

After Emmett's death, Mamie toured the nation with the National Association for the Advancement of Colored People (NAACP), calling for equal rights and raising thousands of dollars for the organization. She then went back to school, graduating cum laude from the Chicago Teachers College, ultimately earning a master's degree in administration and supervision from Loyola University. Mamie spent twenty years teaching elementary classes and special education in the Chicago Public Schools. Along the way she formed a speech and theater group called the Emmett Till Players. They traveled the nation, winning awards with their messages of hope, excellence, and equity. At every opportunity, Mamie continued to share Emmett's story, ensuring that his life and his death would never be forgotten.

In January 2003, Mamie died from a heart condition she had acquired as a child: an enlarged heart with a leaky valve. It is painfully poetic that for most of her eighty-one years Mamie walked the earth with a literal *and* figurative broken heart. Yet her pain did not stop her from living and forgiving. It did not stop her from furthering her education and pouring that love and dedication into other people's children. It did not stop her from giving and receiving love. In fact, Mamie married Mr. Gene Mobley, Emmett's barber, driving coach, and friend, in June of 1957. They remained together until his death in 2000.

Mamie Till-Mobley is an excellent example of resilience and grace. She wrote history with the blood of her son, forcing the world to look race-hatred in the eye and do something about it. It is in honor of this courageous woman that we continue to tell Emmett's story. It is in *Emmett's* honor that we celebrate the person he loved most of all—an incredible daughter, student, educator, activist, advocate, wife, and mother: Mamie Till-Mobley. It is our hope that this book will inspire young people, parents, and educators to— like Mamie—choose voice, choose resilience, and choose brave.

A NOTE ON THE FINAL SPREAD:

The image on the last page of *Choosing Brave* portrays the National Museum of African American History and Culture in Washington, D.C. I was able to visit the museum as part of my research. While there, I sat in a church pew near Emmett's original casket, and I wept. I wept for the terror of Emmett's final hours, calling for his mother and his god. I wept for Mamie as I imagined her grief. But I was also overcome by the thought that this story, the story of a mother being denied justice for her murdered Black son, is *still so relevant*. It's painful to think about. So here, we felt compelled to honor some of those who, like Emmett, fell victim to race-hatred, unreasonable fear, excessive force, and a basic disregard for human life. The list is by no means exhaustive. Sadly, we've come to a place where there are too many modern-day victims to name, yet we grieve them all: men, women, and children who, instead of due process, received a death penalty for everyday living—for playing in the park; purchasing candy; walking down the street; hitchhiking; collecting cans; sleeping in their beds; eating at their tables; reaching for their wallets; listening to music; acting "strangely"; explaining themselves; jogging; waiting for a bus; waiting for an Uber; taking out the trash; selling cigarettes; holding a pipe, a drill, or a cell phone; and attending Bible study. May we remember their stories, say their names, and do all that we can to make "lists of the lost" obsolete.

—Angela Joy

Illustrator's Note

I am honored to be included in telling Mamie Till-Mobley's life story. I first learned about her and Emmett Till in school. I can't recall my age, but I was old enough to understand their importance to American history and that their names would forever be with me. Then, as an adult, I visited the National Museum of African American History and Culture in Washington, D.C., where I tearfully viewed Emmett's glass-topped casket and listened to the audio of Mamie speaking. Mamie was brave, and I could feel her presence at the exhibit still saying, "I wanted the world to see what they did to my baby."

To illustrate a mother's grief and pain, which are what ultimately led her to show Emmett's body to the world, I needed to understand Mamie Till-Mobley more intimately as a person. To accomplish this, I spent hours watching documentaries of the trial, listening to interviews with Mamie and her family, and reading articles about Emmett's funeral. In addition, I collected historical photos of the landscape and people from Mississippi, the Tallahatchie River, and Chicago. Finally, I searched for photographs of Mamie at different ages. However, since her life before the court trial was not documented extensively, I had to envision what she looked like while growing up, how she expressed herself to her family, and how she loved Emmett. I sketched and took pictures from documentaries to help capture Mamie's expressions, which were solemn with small glimpses of joy. This joy would shine through when she spoke of Emmett as a young child and talked about her teaching in Chicago after Emmett's death.

As I was working on this book and learning more about Emmett's death, I saw the parallels with the deaths of George Floyd, Breonna Taylor, and many others. It compelled me to illustrate the fence surrounding Lafayette Square in Washington, D.C., erected in June 2020 to prevent demonstrators from entering the park and protesting in front of the White House. In response, activists turned it into a memorial wall to honor those who lost their lives to injustice. For me, it became an expression of the legacy of Mamie Till-Mobley and Emmett Till that still lives on.

Emmett was killed during the Jim Crow era because he supposedly wolf-whistled to a white woman. A two-note breath of air that brought forth a harsh and swift conviction of this teenage boy. Instead of designing a paper cut of Emmett whistling, I focused on the action itself as a sound wave. I wanted to convey through the simplicity of paper the power and vibrations that this sound carried and continues to carry even after Emmett's death.

Mamie spent her later years teaching and encouraging adults and children, often using speeches by Dr. Martin Luther King Jr. Mamie's students used their voices and energy to uplift their community and bring change. An example of her enduring inspiration is the naming of the Emmett Till Unsolved Civil Rights Act, which funded the investigation of the murder of Alberta Odell Jones. The bill was signed into law in 2008 to address how the justice system has historically failed African Americans and allows government agents to investigate cold cases before 1970 that may be related to civil rights violations. Jones was an attorney who taught African Americans in Louisville, Kentucky, how to use voting machines. She was murdered in 1965, and her case has remained unsolved. Mamie's bravery has also inspired other mothers—like Eric Garner's mother, Gwen Carr—who have become leaders in their communities, advocating on behalf of their children to bring awareness to the need for police reform and accountability from their states' lawmakers.

To create images of Mamie's life, I wove her story using negative and positive spaces by cutting black paper and layering tissue paper underneath to add color. The colors throughout represent skin tone and convey feelings of bravery, sadness, and hope from Mamie and her family. Some of the text in the art was hand-cut. For example, the train station signs that appear on two spreads read, "The City of New Orleans," which is the name of the train Emmett rode to Mississippi and the same train that brought his body back in a coffin to his mother.

Using these techniques, I am confident that Mamie's story of bravery will leave an imprint on your heart, mind, and soul.

—Janelle Washington

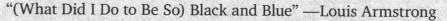

Choosing Brave: The Soundtrack

"(What Did I Do to Be So) Black and Blue" —Louis Armstrong

"Two O'Clock Blues" —Jimmy Yancey

"Black, Brown, and White" —Big Bill Broonzy

"A Mother's Love" —Kem

"City of New Orleans" —Willie Nelson

"My Name Is Emmett Till" —Emmylou Harris

"Take My Hand, Precious Lord" —Mahalia Jackson

"Ain't Gonna Let Nobody Turn Me 'Round" —Sweet Honey in the Rock

"The Death of Emmett Till" —Ben Williams

Tribute to Mamie: "Sadie" —The Spinners

Vocabulary

Buffalo Nickel: A five-cent piece designed with a buffalo on one side and a Native American chief on the other, minted from 1913 to 1938. The designer, James Earle Fraser, used three chiefs to model the image: Iron Tail of the Sioux, Two Moons of the Cheyenne, and John Big Tree of the Seneca Nation. The buffalo pictured is rumored to be Black Diamond, a Barnum & Bailey Circus animal that was given to the Bronx Zoo.

Emmett Till Players: Founded by Mamie-Till Mobley in 1973, the ETP was a group of young people who traveled across the nation delivering the words of Dr. Martin Luther King Jr., inspiring hope for equity, unity, and peace.

The Great Migration (1910–1970): The mass movement of approximately 6 million African Americans from the South to northern cities in search of economic opportunity and physical safety.

Iceman/Milkman: In the early 1900s, electric refrigerators were a rare luxury. Instead, people used iceboxes—wooden compartments lined with insulation to keep perishable items cool. Using ice purchased from the local iceman, families were able to keep their food cool for a day or two. Even with the cooling effect of the icebox, it was still difficult to keep milk from spoiling quickly. For this reason, milkmen were employed to deliver fresh dairy from local farms to front doors every day. The glass bottles were used, collected, cleaned, and reused, creating zero waste.

Jim Crow: Laws and lifestyles that deprived Black people of equal rights, equal access, and equal opportunity. Living in Jim Crow meant that Black people weren't free to choose where they ate, slept, worked, walked, or even where they went to the bathroom. Something as simple as the sale of a toilet paper roll could be denied to Black American citizens under the laws of Jim Crow.

Juke Joint: A pop-up establishment, typically in Black communities, where one can eat, drink, socialize, and dance to the sound of a jukebox or live performance.

Lynching: A mob killing, especially by hanging, for an alleged offense without legal trial.

MoonPie: A popular dessert invented in 1917, a MoonPie is a marshmallow sandwiched between two graham cracker cookies, dipped in chocolate.

Mothers of the Movement: An organization founded in 2013 by African American women whose children have been killed by police or gun violence. They are activists, politicians, public speakers, and community organizers.

NAACP: The National Association for the Advancement of Colored People; an organization created in 1909 to pursue the civil rights of African Americans in the United States.

Polio: A contagious viral illness that can cause nerve injury leading to paralysis, difficulty breathing, and sometimes death. In the late 1940s, when Emmett contracted the disease, polio left over thirty-five thousand people paralyzed each year. A vaccine created in 1955 greatly decreased the number of polio cases in the United States, the last of which was reported in 1979.

Profane: To treat a holy place or object with great disrespect.

Stutter: To speak with continued involuntary repetition of sounds, especially initial consonants.

—————— Time Line of a Crime ——————

Saturday, August 20, 1955—Fourteen-year-old Emmett Till boards a southbound train to visit relatives in Mississippi.

Wednesday, August 24, 1955—Emmett enters Bryant's Grocery and Meat Market to purchase bubble gum. Through the plate-glass window, one witness sees Emmett place his money in the clerk's hand instead of on the counter, violating social codes of conduct for the time and region. The clerk, Carolyn Bryant, leaves the store to get her pistol. Outside,

Emmett is heard making a whistling sound, later called a "wolf whistle," a noise associated with expressing sexual attraction or admiration.

Sunday, August 28, 1955, 2:00 a.m.—Emmett is pulled out of bed and kidnapped from his great-uncle's home. He is beaten, tortured, and murdered. His body is disposed of in the Tallahatchie River, tied to a cotton gin.

Monday, August 29, 1955—The store clerk's husband, Roy Bryant, and his half brother, J. W. Milam, are arrested in connection to Emmett's disappearance.

Wednesday, August 31, 1955—Emmett's body is found.

Thursday, September 1, 1955—In a newspaper report aimed at justifying Emmett's kidnapping, Sheriff George Smith states that the store clerk and her family became "offended when young Till waved to the woman and said 'goodbye.'" Two days later, the sheriff inflated the account, stating that Emmett "made an ugly remark" to the store clerk. These statements, which grew in their severity over time, were used to illustrate Emmett's alleged impropriety.

September 19–23, 1955—Testimony begins in the kidnapping and murder trial of Emmett Till. At great risk to self and family, Moses Wright (Emmett's great-uncle) identifies and testifies against the men who abducted Emmett from his home. The defense calls the store clerk to testify "for the record." Her "recollection" now includes suffering from a physical attack, an attack that was recreated in the courtroom, an attack that Emmett did not have time or opportunity to commit. The clerk returns to her seat without the "burden" of being cross-examined.

An all-white, all-male jury deliberates for just over an hour to return a verdict of not guilty. One juror is recorded saying that they took a soda break to stretch things out—"make it look good." The clerk's husband and half brother, who admitted kidnapping Emmett on the night in question, walk out of the courthouse free.

January 24, 1956—*Look* magazine publishes an interview with the clerk's husband and his half brother. In it, they confess to beating, killing, and dumping Emmett in the Tallahatchie River. Double jeopardy prevents them from being retried for their crimes. They are paid $4,000 for the interview.

December 31, 1980—Acquitted murderer J. W. Milam dies of cancer, age sixty-one.

September 1, 1994—Acquitted murderer Roy Bryant dies of cancer, age sixty-three.

January 6, 2003—Mamie Till-Mobley dies of heart failure, age eighty-one.

2004—The U.S. Justice Department reopens Emmett's murder case.

2005—Emmett's casket is exhumed. His identity is confirmed, and an autopsy is conducted. Due to state laws, a used casket cannot be reburied. A new casket is purchased, and the original makes its circuitous way to the National Museum of African American History and Culture in Washington, D.C., where it stands as an exhibit today.

January 31, 2017—In his book *The Blood of Emmett Till*, journalist Timothy B. Tyson writes that the store clerk who accused Emmett of grabbing her recanted her statement, saying, "That part's not true . . . Nothing that boy did could ever justify what happened to him."

March 7, 2022—Following its passage in the House of Representatives by a vote of 422 to 3, the U.S. Senate unanimously passes the Emmett Till Antilynching Act, making lynching a federal crime. It took over 200 attempts and 100 years for Congress to pass an antilynching bill.

--------- **Sources** ---------

"Buffalo Nickel: 1913–1938 Buffalo Nickel Coin Guide," My Coin Guides, 2020, buffalonickel.org.

★ Burch, Audra D. S., Veda Shastri, and Tim Chaffee. "Emmett Till's Murder, and How America Remembers Its Darkest Moments," *New York Times*, Febuary 20, 2019, nyti.ms/2HRbSRf.

Callard, Abby. "Emmett Till's Casket Goes to the Smithsonian," *Smithsonian Magazine,* November 2009, smithsonianmag.com/arts-culture/emmett-tills-casket-goes-to-the-smithsonian 144696940.

"History of Lynchings," The National Association for the Advancement of Colored People, naacp.org/history-of-lynchings.

Jalon, Allan. "1955 Killing Sparked Civil Rights Revolution: Emmett Till: South's Legend and Legacy," *Los Angeles Times,* October 7, 1985, latimes.com/archives/la-xpm-1985-10-07-mn-16511-story.html.

Mamie Till Mobley Memorial Foundation, mamietillmobleyfoundation.org.

★ "The Murder of Emmett Till," *PBS: American Experience,* pbs.org/wgbh/americanexperience/features/till-timeline.

"Polio Elimination in the United States," Centers for Disease Control and Prevention, cdc.gov/polio/what-is-polio/polio-us.html.

Till-Mobley, Mamie, and Christopher Benson. *Death of Innocence: The Story of the Hate Crime That Changed America*. New York: Random House, 2003.

Tyson, Timothy B. *The Blood of Emmett Till.* New York: Simon & Schuster, 2017.

★ Recommended educators' resource

For my son L. G.,
who, at 14, holds my heart on a string
—A. J.

To my family and memory of my brothers,
Rodney and Tim Hunter, who would be so proud
—J. W.

Published by Roaring Brook Press | Roaring Brook Press is a division of Holtzbrinck Publishing Holdings Limited Partnership | 120 Broadway, New York, NY 10271 mackids.com | Text copyright © 2022 by Angela Joy Seard. | Illustrations copyright © 2022 by Janelle Washington. | All rights reserved. | Our books may be purchased in bulk for promotional, educational, or business use. Please contact your local bookseller or the Macmillan Corporate and Premium Sales Department at (800) 221-7945 ext. 5442 or by email at MacmillanSpecialMarkets@macmillan.com. | Library of Congress Cataloging-in-Publication Data is available. | First edition, 2022 | The illustrations for this book were created by cutting twenty-one sheets of black paper with a craft knife using 71 blades. | Red, blue, and white tissue paper were added to create layers. | The text was set in Charter. The book was edited by Connie Hsu, art directed by Sharismar Rodriguez, and designed by Lisa Vega. The production editors were Starr Baer and Taylor Pitts, and the production manager was Susan Doran. | Printed in China by RR Donnelley Asia Printing Solutions Ltd., Dongguan City, Guangdong Province. ISBN 978-1-250-22095-0 | 10 9 8 7 6 5 4 3